This book is dedicated to...

the memory of Doug McCoy, Speedy Rearden,
Cathey Cashion and Hugh Potts.

my children, Catherine, Patrick and Anna.
You are the keepers of my heart.

my husband, Gary Wright,
whose energy, devotion, support and friendship
provides the balance in my life.

JoAnne Oliver spent her formative years in Memphis, Tennessee and is a graduate of the University of Mississippi. Currently living in Hot Springs, Arkansas, JoAnne thrives as an artist and a writer. *Just Imagine It* is a culmination of her personal journey that she hopes will serve as an instrument to finding inner peace and strength in a world of uncertainties.

If we journey
through life with
the
curiosity of children,
we will never miss
the
playgrounds of opportunity.

Be *flexible* ...

Plan C should always
be an option!

One will never
meet a *perfect* person.

Notice everything & everyone...

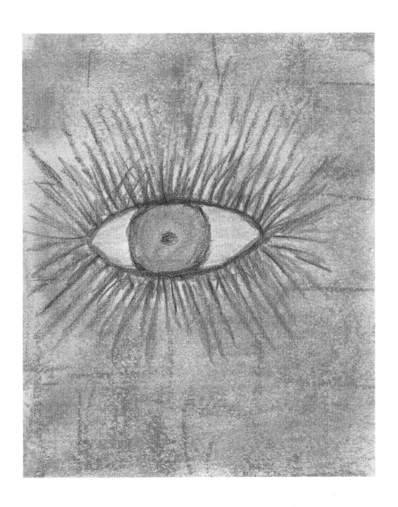

Learning to
love oneself is *bravery*
in its purest form.

Never disappoint your
father
or embarrass your
mother.

One's *education*
is a crucial tool
for building *self-confidence.*

Strive

to

be

consistent...

Store your life's accomplishments
in the *finest* corner
of your soul.

Continuously visualize
the way you want your
life to be.

There might be a time
when each of us
is temporarily insane!

Give *everyone*
the benefit of the doubt.

Address those who
have served our country
and tell them

'thank you.'

Live life as a participant...

You will pass
with flying colors
those things which *interest* you!

No one deserves *criticism*
if it isn't spoken in
a *constructive* tone.

Compliment someone
every day...

Encourage people to
remove their *masks*
and share their *identity* with the world.

Deceit destroys the soul...

Always honor
those who taught you lessons.

Along life's journey,
hold onto your *integrity*.

As your final hour approaches,
you can sign the last scorecard with
honor.

Beware

the

shortcuts

you

take

in

Life!

Fathers give
their children *strength*.

Mothers teach them *compassion*.

Good friends are
the best investments
life offers.

You can give away your heart,
but never, for whatever reason,
give away your soul,
   and you will always have a place
to call *'home.'*

Sarcasm destroys one's mood.

You will probably learn more
valuable lessons
from people who disagree with you than
from those who choose to agree.

Few things are as ridiculously exhilarating as *falling in love*!

Artists give people
the wonderful opportunity
to visually relive their lives.

A special freedom occurs within the mind when you learn to *love your body.*

This freedom *unlocks* the prison door to your soul.

A *firm handshake* is a sure sign of *character*.

In the game of Life,

play fair...

Always be willing
to
take a chance...

Choose

to

be

important...

The happiest people
are those with
open minds and forgiving hearts.

Always have *something*
to be excited about.

Confidence is the *electricity* of the soul...

Shining knights *can't* see through your armor.

Not

everything

has

an

answer...

It is terribly disappointing
not to be heard.

Never underestimate the
load you can carry.

A *mother's love* is as *constant* as the sunrise.

Every once in a while,
stand

in

the

pouring

rain!

If we placed a price tag on
the *adverse experiences* in our lifetime,
those who learned to use them as
stepping stones
would amass great wealth.

Those who used them as *stumbling blocks*
would end their journey poverty stricken.

Discipline
is something worth practicing
every day.

*How powerful
the presence of a confident
woman...*

You shouldn't stare at people without a *smile* on your face.

Life is all about choices;
therefore, choose to stay on the
balance beam

rather than the
tight rope.

Curiosity is the foundation of knowledge.

When *appropriate*,
always be willing to
express your opinions.

Anticipation takes you
back to the innocent and honest
feelings of *childhood*.

One can find a
best friend *anywhere*.

Be on time...

You will always feel lonely
if you can't *love* and *respect* that
face in the mirror.

Apologies are usually
an opportunity for *growth*.

They might be the *looking glass*
into one's soul.

Be adaptive.

Change allows one to reach their *full* potential.

Parenthood
is the *greatest complexity* in life...

Intelligence isn't nearly as beneficial as *pure common sense*.

When the thorns of life strike, common sense keeps one moving in a forward direction instead of pausing to analyze the data.

Loneliness devours the soul...

There is *one* thing
mankind has in common:

Each of us is a *teacher*
whether we choose to be or not.

Teach children
　　　the *positive* effects of *change*
and they will become
　　　more *open-minded* adults.

Manipulative people
are like puppets.

They journey through life with
too many strings attached.

A *smile* can unlock someone's world.

Unless something is *life-threatening*, don't let it spoil your day.

Pity the person who
   never learned to say, *'I'm sorry'.*

Encouragement
strengthens
the spirit...

Concentrate on keeping
 your life *simplified*.

(The result will be astounding.)

My grandmother's motto:

'We all fall short.'

Bitterness is the

deadliest virus.

Beware the *perfectionist*.
(They are only *half* alive.)

A part of knowledge is
the remembrance of things
one has forgotten!

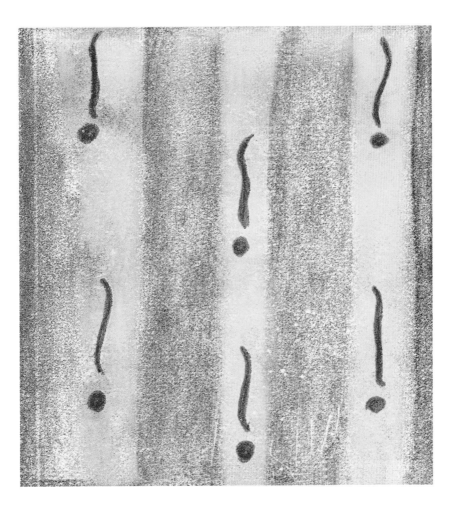

Watch carefully...

opportunity often passes in a flash.

Get up as often
as possible to watch
the sunrise.

By *communicating* with people,
you open yourself to being
surrounded by hugs
everyday of your life.

Remember:
There is *never* a reason
to allow yourself to be
intimidated by *anyone*.

Be cautious...
The 'Boogie-man'
 is still out there.

Everything is a state of mind.

(That can be *changed* if necessary.)

Everyone we encounter
will tell us an interesting story
                if we ask them to share one.

The problem is that *too few ask*.

Begin the things you *least* enjoy with a *sense of humor!*

*N*ever complain.

(The grass isn't greener
on the other side.)

Worry
          is
              sinful.

The best medicine is
a *strong embrace*.

I have never met *anyone*
    with whom I would swap lives.

Integrity and *self-esteem* are the *essential* parts of character one must possess to *survive* life's hurdles.

Miracles *do* happen.

Compliments
exhilarate people.
They are priceless treasurers.

Life becomes boring
when we cease to
challenge ourselves.

Be careful.
Boredom can rob your
spirit of rejuvenation.

Sometimes it helps to
prepare yourself
to expect the unexpected!

Better run
* as fast as you can*
from the pessimist...

Make use of the time
you spend waiting in lines
by counting your blessings and praying
for those around you.

Pace yourself...

Understand *the difference* between

knowledge and wisdom.

Lead an exemplary life.

(*Someone's* watching.)

Surround yourself
    with people that love you.

Life is not a battle zone.

It is a *playground*.

Watch out...
Don't become too obsessed
with your possessions.

U-hauls *don't* follow hearses.

Every once in a while,

take off

and run as fast as you can.

The more *choices*,
however simple one allows their
children to have,
the more prolific *decision makers*
they will become as adults.

It is *vitally* important
to keep your *chin up*
through the difficult times
when life deals you a *nosebleed!*

Energy is the *soul's fuel*.

Save it for yourself rather than
wasting its force
trying to understand the actions and
decisions of others.

The 11th Commandment:
Thou shalt not procrastinate!

The 12th Commandment:

Thou shalt not be incompetent.

God answers prayer
in three ways:

1. yes
2. no
3. *not yet*

If someone seeks forgiveness, grant it.

If one doesn't ask, forgive them anyway.

Remember this:

Men do not *look* like
think like
act like
or
feel like women.

Never, for whatever reason,
outgrow being a
cheerleader.

Learn to live with a
sense of contentment
because life is skipping on past
as if its in a hurry to go some
place it hasn't been before.

My grandmother was firmly convinced
all of the evil acts
committed were a direct result of a
person never feeling loved.

Age and observation have convinced
me she was right.

*Stand
firm*
in
the
things
you
believe
in.

Life is one gigantic *training school.*
The more intently you *observe*
and *listen,*
the fewer notes
you need bother taking.

Church steeples are often seen
in the middle of *nowhere*
to remind us that God is
Everywhere.

Approach life with
your arms *open*,
your head *clear*,
and
your feet *grounded*.

Take lots of joy rides!

joy Rides

I feel sorry for those who view *parenthood* as a *hobby*, for their children grow up feeling used.

I feel sad for those who view *parenthood* as an *occupation*. Their children grow up feeling the need to stay busy.

Be prepared.

Say, 'I love you.'

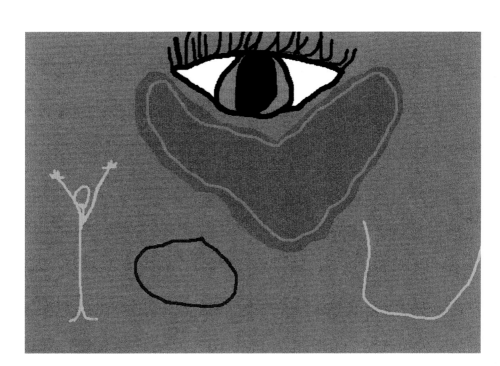

Take advantage of *every* experience offered
so you can always say,

'I'm glad I did,'
rather than
'I wish I had.'

Volunteer.

Leave a trail.